TALKING TO GOD

God Help

Delia Tombleson
ILLUSTRATED BY
Diane Matthes

God help me in my home
A loving child to be,

And help my Mum
and Dad
Who work so hard
for me.

When I'm with other children
Make me a good,
kind friend,

And help me in our games
To share things and to lend.

God help me not be naughty
When I am tired from play,

Help me listen to
my parents
Who show me the
right way.

God help me love all creatures
And treat them all with care,

God help me to remember
To talk to you in prayer.

God help me be your child
The whole of my life through,